FIND IT!

A BIG BOOK OF SEEK-AND-FIND ADVENTURES

This amazing book is packed with things to find and puzzles to solve!
Read the instructions to complete each activity and then
turn to the back of the book to check the answers.
Answers are grouped by activity type to help you find them.
Have fun!

*make
believe
ideas*

THE JOLLY JUNGLE

The jungle is fun to explore – until you get lost! The poor explorer is trying to get home before dark, especially now that one naughty animal has taken his supplies!

Scan the scene and search for:

- a banana
- a dragonfly
- 8 frogs
- 7 hungry fish
- a leopard
- 6 snakes
- a spotted beak
- a statue
- a swimmer
- a white bird

MATCH THE PAIRS!

Draw lines to **JOIN** the matching **PAIRS AT THE BEACH**.
Can you find the **FIVE** matching pairs?

WHO ATE BUILDER BILL'S LUNCH?

Let's **FIND** who did it! **LOOK** at the list below and **CROSS OUT** the people who **DON'T** have each feature. Keep going until you have **ONE** person left — that's the **CULPRIT!**

The culprit has all of these features:

1. hard hat
2. glasses
3. red shirt
4. black hair
5. clipboard

STEPH PETER HUGH BRAD GRANT

SIMON TIM JARED MATTHEW RYAN

DAN BERT HAMISH LUKE DAVE

ROBERTA MALCOLM DARIUS RUPERT BART

FOUND IT!

The culprit is ....

FIND THE DIFFERENCES!

Can you **FIND ALL FIVE DIFFERENCES** between the two pictures? Circle the differences on the right-hand page.

I can be heavy; I can be light.
Take me home or on a flight.

A = ♥
B = ♫
C = ★
D = ✔
E = ✉
F = ⚙
G = 🏠
H = 🔒
I = 🚩
J = 📕
K = 🎁
L = 🧰
M = 📌
N = ✅
O = 🔨
P = 🚚
Q = 🌍
R = ✂
S = 🍴
T = ✈
U = ⚓
V = 🔧
W = 🔔
X = 🗑
Y = 🚀
Z = ↺

CODE BREAKER

Now use the symbol chart to break
the code and find the answer:

🍴 🚚 🔨 ✂ ✈ 🍴   ♫ ♥ 🏠

_____ ___

DIGGING DISCOVERY

These busy builders have dug up more than they bargained for! Can you identify the skeleton before a naughty pup steals the bones?

Scan the scene and search for:

- 3 apples
- a ball
- 4 birds
- a cement truck
- a clipboard
- 8 cones
- a dog
- a lunchbox
- a pile of bricks
- a walkie-talkie

CAMOUFLAGED CREATURES!

Can you **FIND 10 LEOPARDS** hidden in the pattern?

FINDING FOSSILS!

```
n y u m w r g c j z g q e r w
o f m b d o b i l w d y i d f
u q a v z c n x p i e w o i f
u a q e s k b n t q q g p n y
m e e n a j r i e y f v s o t
u r i f l t o t r m b z t s r
t a j f w e n r o a o e e a i
t p c y a e t e d o n r g u c
v t f a e t o x a c e g o r e
o o g n v h s n c d e s s h r
l r t s b e a d t l w l a g a
c y u i y i u z y a k n u f t
a k e s c e r j l k r u r g o
n m w b b m u c y o x n u m p
o h k b h h s d h c t k s x s
```

SEARCH the grid to FIND all the FOSSILIZED words below.

bone	dinosaur	raptor	tree
brontosaurus	egg	rock	t.rex
cave	horn	stegosaurus	triceratops
claws	pterodactyl	teeth	volcano

STRANGE SAFARI!

Find **FIVE THINGS** that **DON'T BELONG.**

FOUND IT! The five things that don't belong are:

1. _____
2. _____
3. _____
4. _____
5. _____

BAGS OF FUN!

It's nearly time to go on a trip — where would you like to fly? We better get going before this very full bag bursts!

Scan the scene and search for:

- 8 flowers
- a giraffe
- a gorilla
- a grasshopper
- a hamster
- a hyena
- an iguana
- a jellyfish
- a kangaroo
- a koala

FIND THE DIFFERENCES!

"FIND IT" BY RYAN CHAMPNISS

"FIND IT" BY RYAN CHAMPNISS

EARN YOUR STRIPES!

Find **FIVE** animals that are disguised as **TIGERS**.

FOUND IT! The 5 animals are:

1.   2.   3.   4.   5.

FOLLOW THE TRAILS!

HELP the **DINOSAUR** choose the right trail to get to the **CAVE.**

I SCREAM FOR ICE CREAM!

FIND the picture that answers the SUM.

CAMOUFLAGED CREATURES!

Can you FIND 10 ZEBRAS hidden in the pattern?

LARRY THE LION HAS LOST HIS PRIDE!

Larry's pride is **HIDDEN** under one of the things on the **SAFARI MAP**. Solve the **RIDDLE**, then circle where you **THINK** you will find the pride.

RIDDLE

I'm not planning a trip away,
but I carry a trunk every day!

CODE BREAKER

Now use the symbol chart to break
the code and find the answer:

A = ♥
B = ♫
C = ★
D = ✔
E = ✉
F = ⚙
G = 🏠
H = 🔒
I = 🚩
J = 📕
K = 🎁
L = 💼
M = 📌
N = ✅
O = 🔨
P = 🚚
Q = 🌐
R = ✂
S = 🍴
T = 🚀
U = ⚓
V = 🔧
W = 🔔
X = 🗑
Y = 🚀
Z = ↺

HIDDEN TREASURE!

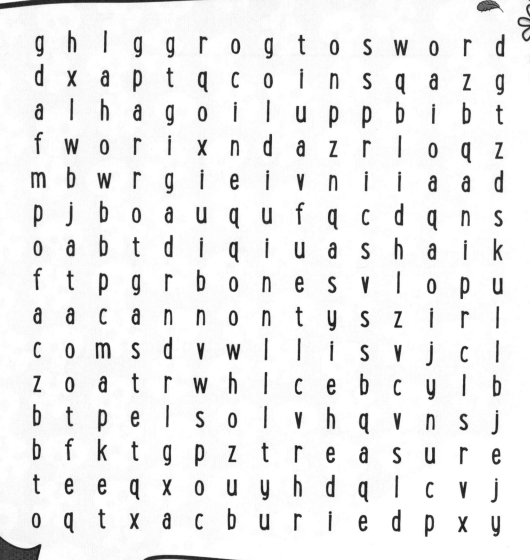

```
g h l g g r o g t o s w o r d
d x a p t q c o i n s q a z g
a l h a g o i l u p p b i b t
f w o r i x n d a z r l o q z
m b w r g i e i v n i i a a d
p j b o a u q u f q c d q n s
o a b t d i q i u a s h a i k
f t p g r b o n e s v l o p u
a a c a n n o n t y s z i r l
c o m s d v w l l i s v j c l
z o a t r w h l c e b c y l b
b t p e l s o l v h q v n s j
b f k t g p z t r e a s u r e
t e e q x o u y h d q l c v j
o q t x a c b u r i e d p x y
```

SEARCH the grid to FIND all the PIRATE'S words below.

anchor	cannon	gold	plank
boat	captain	island	skull
bones	coins	map	sword
buried	flag	parrot	treasure

Draw lines to JOIN the matching PAIRS OF ANIMALS. Can you find all FIVE matching pairs?

MOTOR MADNESS

The race is about to begin! The crowd is cheering, the engines are humming, and some chickens are crossing the road — I wonder why . . .

Scan the scene and search for:

- an alien
- an apple
- a bucket
- 7 chickens
- 12 cones
- a flashlight
- 2 green cowboys
- 3 hammers
- a horse
- a screwdriver

FIND THE DIFFERENCES!

Can you **FIND ALL FIVE DIFFERENCES** between the two pictures? Circle the differences on the right-hand page.

FOUND IT! The five things that don't belong are:

① 1. ② 2. ③ 3. ④ 4. ⑤ 5.

WHO ATE ALL THE PET FOOD?

Let's **FIND** who did it! **LOOK** at the list below and **CROSS OUT** the animals who **DON'T** have each feature. Keep going until you have **ONE** animal left — that's the **CULPRIT!**

The culprit has all of these features:

1. spots
2. collar
3. bow
4. feathers
5. yellow beak

 REX

 FIDO

 TIGGER

 THUMPER

 GREENIE

 MR OINK

 PENNY

 POLLY

 QUACKER

 FLUFFY

 ELVIS

 BRUNO

 FRANK

 WHISKERS

 SPOT

 CURLY

 PINKY

 WADDLE

 ROSIE

 CHARLOTTE

FOUND IT!

The culprit is ....

COUNTRY CHAOS

Everyone is having fun in the country — except for one poor critter, who's in a little bit of trouble!

Scan the scene and search for:

- 5 black-and-white cows
- 2 brown cows
- 2 cats
- 3 chickens
- 3 cyclists
- 6 dogs
- 4 firemen
- 6 green balloons
- 1 parachutist
- 2 planes

RIDDLE ME THIS!

A THIEF HAS ESCAPED!

The thief is **HIDING** in one of the things on the **TOWN MAP**. Solve the **RIDDLE**, then circle where you **THINK** the thief is hiding.

RIDDLE

Each room of mine has lots of beds.
Sick people come to rest their heads.

A = ♥
B = ♫
C = ★
D = ✔
E = ✉
F = ⚙
G = 🏠
H = 🔒
I = 🚩
J = 📕
K = 🎁
L = 💼
M = 📌
N = ✅
O = 🔨
P = 🚚
Q = 🌍
R = ✂
S = 🍴
T = 🚀
U = ⚓
V = 🔧
W = 🔔
X = 🗑
Y = 🚀
Z = ↺

CODE BREAKER

Now use the symbol chart to break
the code and find the answer:

🔒 🔨 🍴 🚚 🚩 🚀 ♥ 💼

_____

MAJESTIC MAZE

FIND a way through the **MAZE** to help the **PRINCE** get to the **PRINCESS**. Try to pick up the **JEWELS** on the way!

START

FINISH

SEEING STRIPES!

Find **FIVE** animals that are disguised as **ZEBRAS**.

FOUND IT! The 5 animals are:

1. 2. 3. 4. 5.

FIND THE DIFFERENCES!

FARMYARD FUN!

```
d  b  t  g  r  k  m  b  a  r  n  n  f  n  r
y  k  t  t  v  t  v  m  c  t  e  w  f  t  w
f  i  s  t  a  b  l  e  s  k  c  a  q  o  s
a  g  t  q  c  a  a  e  c  g  s  u  r  a  h
r  i  a  j  h  o  v  i  l  e  a  c  w  w  e
m  c  l  p  x  r  h  j  l  e  e  a  y  i  e
e  x  l  g  a  c  k  b  z  r  p  t  c  p  p
r  o  i  h  t  v  a  w  a  r  i  t  o  n  d
z  t  o  r  d  t  r  c  s  o  g  l  t  i  o
f  d  n  u  e  z  s  k  w  l  s  e  r  i  g
g  q  e  g  g  m  e  a  d  o  w  p  a  e  l
s  h  e  p  h  e  r  d  a  p  k  d  c  n  q
u  v  i  k  c  a  e  u  l  a  m  d  t  m  h
d  u  x  g  e  e  v  r  x  o  q  c  o  r  n
c  g  o  o  s  e  t  l  o  v  x  n  r  a  s
```

SEARCH the grid to FIND all the FARMYARD words below.

barn	farmer	pigs	stables
cattle	goose	scarecrow	stallion
chicken	harvest	sheepdog	tractor
corn	meadow	shepherd	vegetables

MATCH THE PAIRS!

Draw lines to **JOIN** the matching
PAIRS OF SEA CREATURES.
Can you find all **FIVE** matching pairs?

CAMOUFLAGED CREATURES!

Can you FIND 10 TIGERS hidden in the pattern?

AHOY, THERE!

It's a very windy day at sea, and the coast guard has to keep a careful lookout — especially for sharks!

Scan the scene and search for:

- 7 beach balls
- 5 dogs
- a ferry
- a fisherman
- a lifesaver ring
- a pirate ship
- 5 seagulls
- 2 shark fins
- a scuba diver
- a sunbather

MECHANIC MIKE HAS LOST HIS HAMMER!

Mike's hammer is HIDDEN under one of the things on the GARAGE MAP. Solve the RIDDLE, then circle where you THINK you will find the hammer.

POLICE

FIND 17

RIDDLE

I come when you sound the alarm.
My job is to keep you safe from harm.

A = ♥
B = ♪
C = ★
D = ✔
E = ✉
F = ⚙
G = 🏠
H = 🔒
I = 🚩
J = 📕
K = 🎁
L = 💼
M = 📌
N = ✅
O = 🔨
P = 🚚
Q = 🌐
R = ✂
S = 🍴
T = 🚀
U = ⚓
V = 🔧
W = 🔔
X = 🗑
Y = 🚀
Z = ↺

CODE BREAKER

Now use the symbol chart to break
the code and find the answer:

_____

FIND THE DIFFERENCES!

Can you **FIND ALL FIVE DIFFERENCES** between the two pictures? Circle the differences on the right-hand page.

CAMOUFLAGED CREATURES!

Can you FIND 10 DALMATIANS hidden in the pattern?

FIND a way through the MAZE to help the ROCKET get to EARTH. Try not to bump into the COMETS on the way!

ROCKET RACE

START

FINISH

CLOTHING COLLECTION

Before we bring in all the dry clothes, let's make sure there aren't any busy bugs hiding in the underpants!

Scan the scene and search for:

- a dress
- 5 red flowers
- a robot
- 3 sharks
- 2 snails
- a spider
- a tie
- 3 underpants
- a unicorn
- a volcano

SOMETHING'S FISHY!

Find **FIVE** animals that are disguised as spotted **FISH**.

FOUND IT! The 5 animals are:

1. 2. 3. 4. 5.

MIGHTY MACHINES!

```
m x s m i r r o r t y v s d l
m e c h a n i c o r g u j r t
w t x v l j l v u y f c a i s
h o p e q c a r k b u n w v p
w a r z j t q z d n e u k e a
g g m k u l n p w l h k r t
z y j m s t o o l b o x h p n
b t c u e h o f k l s x m e
v l a u s r o u e m u s u l r
b g r v t e m p r t u x x f o
w p w n w w t r u c k a s f i
h r a y w o m n d p x d v j x
e o s y b h r u i s c o n e o
e a h j v e h i c l e g c y c
l d d o v o v e o i l l s g v
```

WORD SEARCH

SEARCH the grid to FIND all the MECHANIC'S words below.

axle	driver	mirror	truck
car	fuel	oil	vehicle
carwash	hammer	road	wheel
cone	mechanic	toolbox	workshop

RIDDLE ME THIS!

PRINCESS PIPPA HAS LOST HER TIARA!

Princess Pippa's tiara is HIDDEN under one of the things on the KINGDOM MAP. Solve the RIDDLE, then circle where you THINK you will find the tiara.

RIDDLE

No stars and moon come out for me, but a braver man you won't see!

CODE BREAKER

Now use the symbol chart to break the code and find the answer:

🎁 ✅ ⚑ 🏠 🔒 🚀

_____ _____ _____ _____ _____ _____

A = ♥
B = ♪
C = ★
D = ✔
E = ✉
F = ⚙
G = 🏠
H = 🔒
I = ⚑
J = 📕
K = 🎁
L = 💼
M = 📌
N = ✅
O = 🔨
P = 🚚
Q = 🌍
R = ✂
S = 🍴
T = 🚀
U = ⚓
V = 🔧
W = 🔔
X = 🗑
Y = 🚀
Z = ↺

FIND THE DIFFERENCES!

Can you **FIND ALL FIVE DIFFERENCES** between the two pictures? Circle the differences on the right-hand page.

WATERY WORLD

The aquarium is packed with cool creatures, but watch out for the snapping sharks because they BITE!

Scan the scene and search for:

- 3 clown fish
- 3 crabs
- 2 eels
- 4 jellyfish
- 2 octopuses
- 3 puffer fish
- 5 starfish
- 5 stingrays
- 5 sea horses
- 3 turtles

ROUND THE BEND!

Find **FIVE THINGS** that **DON'T BELONG.**

FOUND IT! The five things that don't belong are:

1.   2.   3.   4.   5.

FIND THE DIFFERENCES!

Can you **FIND ALL FIVE DIFFERENCES** between the two pictures? Circle the differences on the right-hand page.

CAMOUFLAGED CREATURES!

Can you FIND 10 BUGS hidden in the pattern?

SEE THE SITES!

```
w a l l q k c e m e n t j m e
t f a i a c r a n e n r a n v
f g t b h o f f g h u o h i
d z j u t y t e o l f c o q v
i t x l x v o l r c h k g s f
b i q l s g o e e r j w a j s
u q o d e u l c m b i t w l o
i t d o x p s t a k o y c y b
l l u z c p l r n h p x r f r
d a m e a b r i c k s u v t c
i d p r v b r c q r l b g b w
n d e m a a s i e v y n w q t
g e r x t m z a m i x e r c t
q r o x o k q n z e j q u k w
g m j l r o l l e r v x r r v
```

SEARCH the grid to FIND
all the BUILDER'S words below.

bricks
building
bulldozer
cement

cone
crane
dumper
electrician

excavator
foreman
ladder
mixer

roller
tools
truck
wall

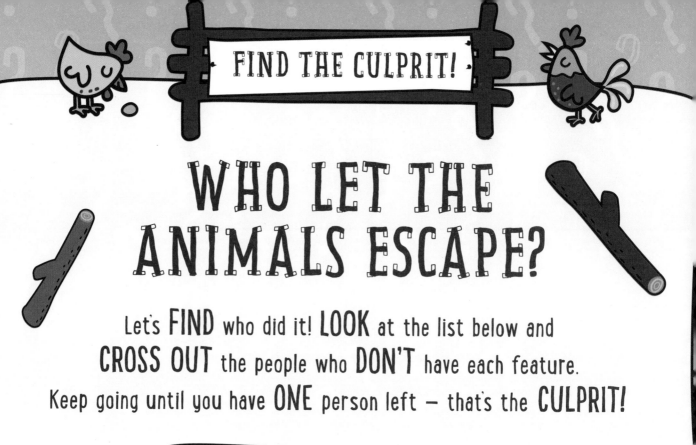

WHO LET THE ANIMALS ESCAPE?

Let's **FIND** who did it! **LOOK** at the list below and **CROSS OUT** the people who **DON'T** have each feature. Keep going until you have **ONE** person left — that's the **CULPRIT!**

The culprit has all of these features:

1. apple
2. spotted boots
3. blue overalls
4. hat
5. facial hair

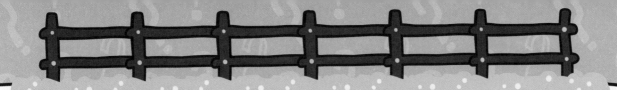

BOBBY

GREG

MATT

JACK

ANETA

CHARLES

RICKY

ANNIE

SARAH

HARVEY

DANIEL

BEN

JOE

ELLIE

MIKEY

PIP

BECKY

JEFF

CRAIG

OLIVIA

FOUND IT!

The culprit is ....

TOY BOX CHALLENGE

The toy box is filled with tiny treasures, but everything has been put away carelessly! Can you find a toy you like?

Scan the scene and search for:

- an anchor
- 2 elephants
- a flag
- a fox
- the letter Z
- 4 stars
- a tiny tiger
- a wand
- 2 whales
- 3 worms

MATCH THE PAIRS!

Draw lines to JOIN the matching PAIRS OF TOYS. Can you find all FIVE matching pairs?

WHO IS MOO?

Find **FIVE** animals that are disguised as **COWS**.

FOUND IT! The 5 animals are:

1.
2.
3.
4.
5.

CUPCAKE CONFUSION!

FIND the picture that answers the SUM.

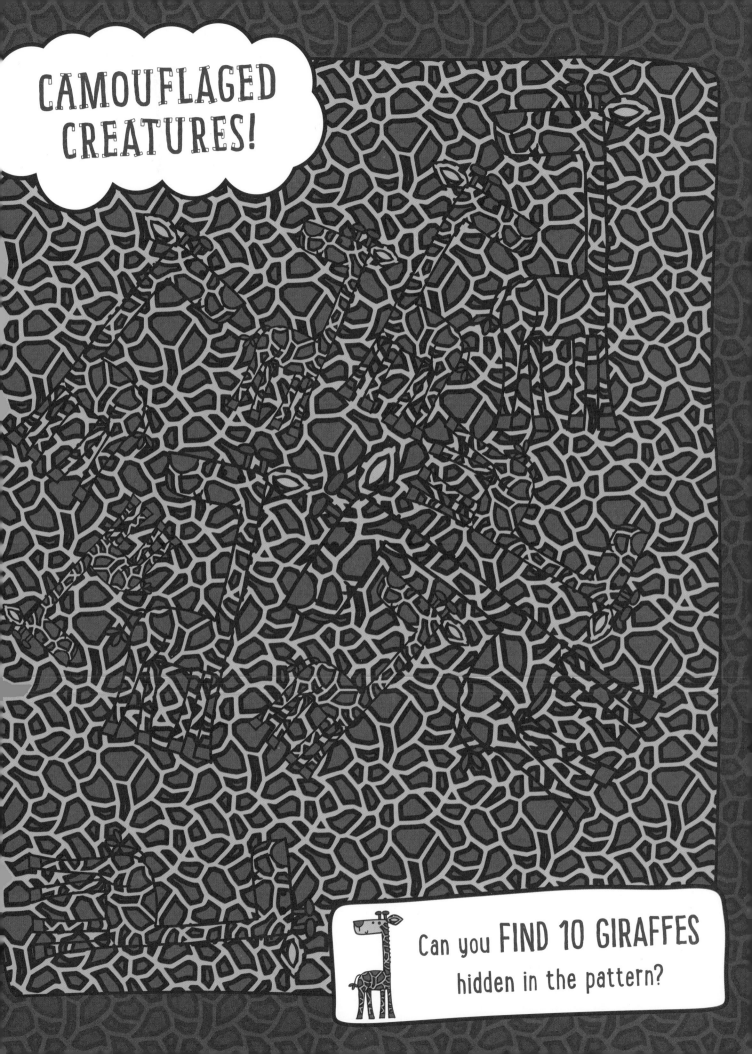

CAMOUFLAGED CREATURES!

Can you FIND 10 GIRAFFES hidden in the pattern?

FOLLOW THE TRAILS!

HELP the PIRATE choose the right trail to get to the TREASURE.

MATCH THE PAIRS!

Draw lines to **JOIN** the matching **PAIRS OF SOCKS.** Can you find all **FIVE** matching pairs?

HIGH-FLYERS

The sky is full of high-flyers! Some people fly fast, some glide, and some brave souls jump out of planes!

Scan the scene and search for:

- 4 airships
- a bird
- a dog
- a flower
- a glider
- 11 green balloons
- 4 hot-air balloons
- a spaceship
- a star
- an upside-down plane

FIND THE DIFFERENCES!

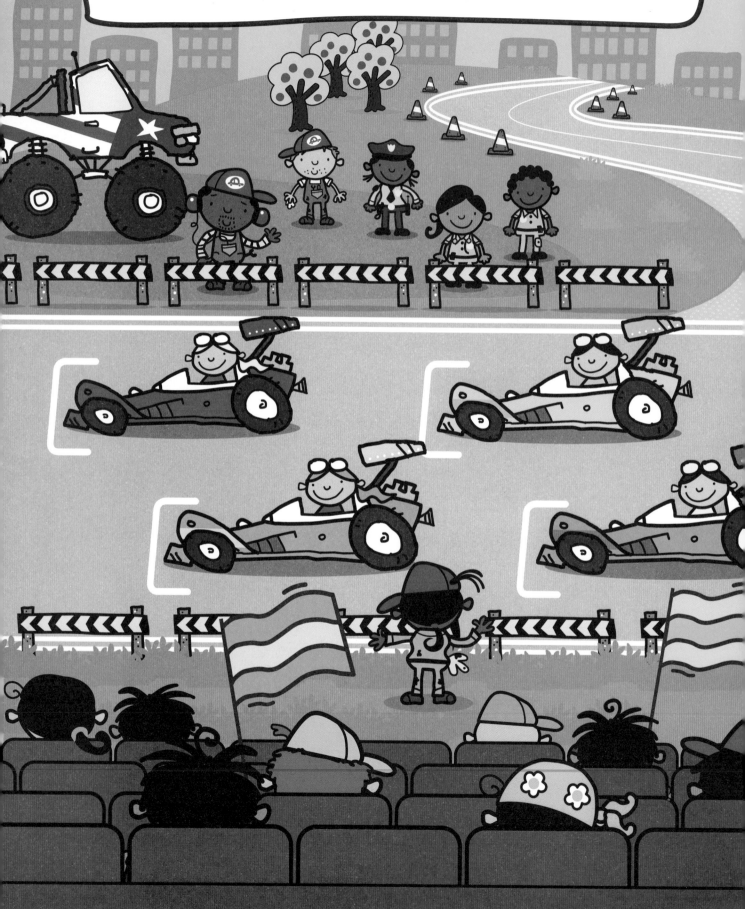

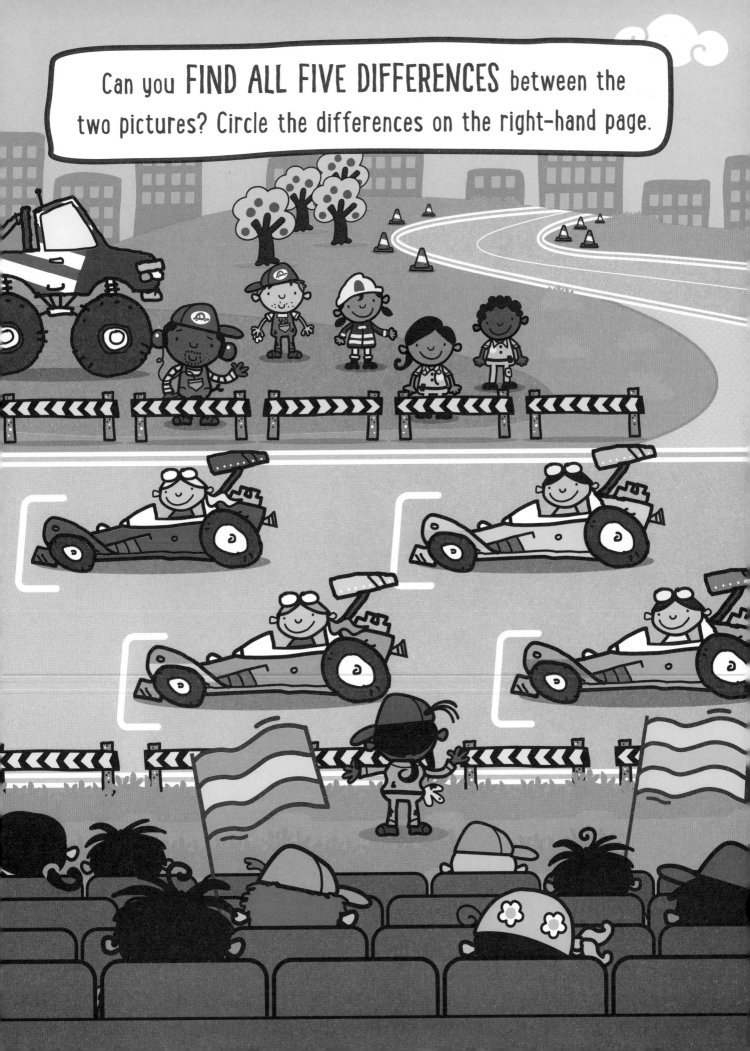

Can you **FIND ALL FIVE DIFFERENCES** between the two pictures? Circle the differences on the right-hand page.

RIDDLE ME THIS!

THE POLAR BEAR HAS LOST HER CUB!

The polar bear's cub is HIDDEN under one of the things on the POLAR MAP. Solve the RIDDLE, then circle where you THINK you will find the cub.

Even though I'm made of snow,
I can keep you warm, you know!

A = ❤
B = 🎵
C = ★
D = ✔
E = ✉
F = ⚙
G = 🏠
H = 🔒
I = 🚩
J = 📕
K = 🎁
L = 💼
M = 📌
N = ✅
O = 🔨
P = 🚚
Q = 🌐
R = ✂
S = 🍴
T = ✈
U = ⚓
V = 🔧
W = 🔔
X = 🗑
Y = 🚀
Z = ↺

CODE BREAKER

Now use the symbol chart to break
the code and find the answer:

___ ___ ___ ___ ___

LAKESIDE LOUNGERS

There's lots to see and do by this beautiful lake. Would you take a dip in the water or fly high for a great view?

Scan the scene and search for:

- a bandana
- 3 bicycles
- a crocodile
- 4 dogs
- 4 flags
- 6 oars
- a periscope
- 2 swimmers
- 2 windsurfers
- 2 yellow birds

SEARCHING SPACE!

```
n j u p i t e r n a p r t s i
t w t a k s g i g p n v e c b
f i m e t e o r a b c s b s z
d a s t r o n a u t u s t a r
c o n s t e l l a t i o n t c
o b s v d e e g e e w x w e z
h o u b k u r n b n a n j l k
e j p w x a a n o u p o c l i
f e e o o l h o o p s c t i b
f t r a p i m n r r a e a t b
g o n p j e f q a l k m a e e
c r o m f n b m u c m t x u d
k b v h h q o b o o s x w i h
v i a a s t e r o i d v k u l
l t t n o n a p s g a l a x y
```

SEARCH the grid to FIND all the ASTRONAUT'S words below.

alien	galaxy	moon	rocket
asteroid	jupiter	nebula	satellite
astronaut	mars	orbit	star
constellation	meteor	planet	supernova

ROCKING RABBITS!

FIND the picture that answers the SUM.

FIND THE DIFFERENCES!

Can you **FIND ALL FIVE DIFFERENCES** between the two pictures? Circle the differences on the right-hand page.

MATCH THE PAIRS!

Draw lines to **JOIN** the matching **PAIRS OF ANIMALS**. Can you find all **FIVE** matching pairs?

IT'S A DOG'S LIFE!

Find **FIVE** animals that are disguised as **DOGS**.

FOUND IT! The 5 animals are:

1.

2.

3.

4.

5.

BEDTIME BONANZA

Molly has spent all day making this big mess and now she's ready for bed. Let's help her clean her room!

Scan the scene and search for:

- a monster
- 3 necklaces
- the number 10
- 16 pandas
- 10 pencils
- a pig
- a pirate
- a queen
- a rocket
- 7 sheep

MISSION TO THE MOON!

Find **FIVE THINGS** that **DON'T BELONG.**

FOUND IT! The five things that don't belong are:

① 　　　② 　　　③ 　　　④ 　　　⑤

FIND THE CULPRIT!

WHO LEFT THE GARAGE IN SUCH A MESS?

Let's **FIND** who did it! **LOOK** at the list below and **CROSS OUT** the people who **DON'T** have each feature. Keep going until you have **ONE** person left – that's the **CULPRIT!**

The culprit has all of these features:

1. cap
2. blue overalls
3. yellow shirt
4. facial hair
5. screwdriver

F1ND 17

GEORGE   RINGO   PAUL   JOHN   HARRY

ZANE   NIALL   LIAM   LOUIS   BRIAN

FREDDIE   NICOLE   RODGER   MIKE   KIM

BARRY   RACHEL   DOUG   ANTHONY   ED

FOUND IT!

The culprit is ....

ROW YOUR BOAT

It's a sunny day in the park and a canoe race is in full swing — but one little sailor is getting in the way!

Scan the scene and search for:

- 2 airships
- 5 balls
- 1 bandana
- 2 cars
- 7 cows
- 3 flowers
- 5 oars
- 2 pink spotted boots
- 1 rosette
- 9 sheep

CLOTHING CALCULATION!

FIND the picture that answers the **SUM**.

WONDERFUL WINGS

Find **FIVE** animals that are disguised as **BUTTERFLIES**.

FOUND IT! The 5 animals are:

1.

2.

3.

4.

5.

PERFECT PALACE!

```
p k z a z n t v f c z n s h m
h i w e l p k i j r s s i c g
d n u e s e r i a d o c q s m
k g e u t a e i n r u g f q o
a d u c z b n o n g a a i u m
v o n s l c m z i c s b n e f
e m b w b a r l c a e r a e p
n z w y i r e w q j o c z n r
y v z d w r p n j c o m c r i
y t i c u i l r i e u r q k n
c p o n y a e n t j z c r x c
y e h j v g u c r o w n c i e
t b t o m e t f z e w d h t s
h b a l l t h r o n e e n c s
o r p r c a s t l e k j r f e
```

SEARCH the grid to **FIND** all the **PRINCESS'S** words below.

ball	diamonds	pony	throne
carriage	frog	prince	tiara
castle	king	princess	tower
crown	kingdom	queen	unicorn

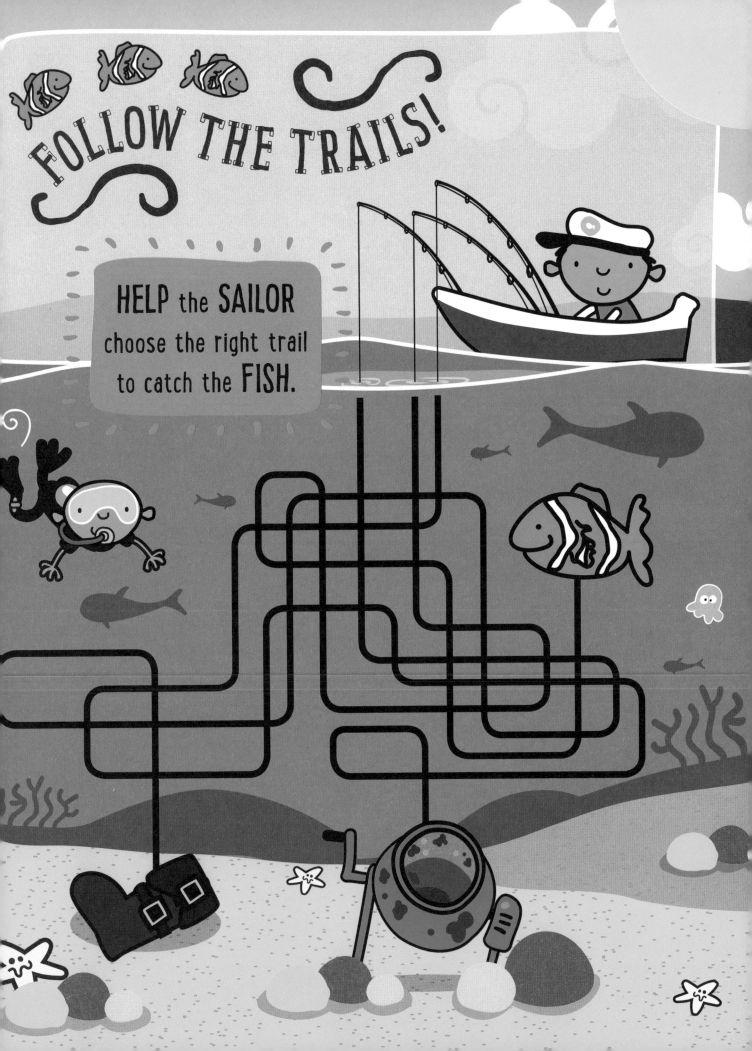

FOLLOW THE TRAILS!

HELP the **SAILOR** choose the right trail to catch the **FISH.**

RIDDLE ME THIS!

DINO DAVE IS LOOKING FOR FOOD!

Dave's food is **HIDDEN** under one of the things on the **PREHISTORIC MAP**. Solve the **RIDDLE**, then circle where you **THINK** you will find the food.

Up to the sky is where I go,
but stand back for I might blow!

A = ♥
B = ♫
C = ★
D = ✔
E = ✉
F = ⚙
G = 🏠
H = 🔒
I = ⚑
J = 📙
K = 🎁
L = 💼
M = 📌
N = ✅
O = 🔨
P = 🚚
Q = 🌐
R = ✂
S = 🍴
T = ✈
U = ⚓
V = 🔧
W = 🔔
X = 🗑
Y = 🚀
Z = ↺

CODE BREAKER

Now use the symbol chart to break
the code and find the answer:

🔧 🔨 💼 ★ ♥ ✅ 🔨

___ ___ ___ ___ ___ ___ ___

AROUND TOWN

All the emergency services are hard at work, but they need some help to find their way around town!

Scan the scene and search for:

- 10 apples
- a bank robber
- a cat in trouble
- a dog
- 5 ducks
- a fast driver
- 4 fire trucks
- an injured person
- 5 paramedics
- 3 police motorcycles

UNDERWATER UNDERCOVER!

Find **FIVE THINGS** that **DON'T BELONG.**

FOUND IT! The five things that don't belong are:

1.   2.   3.   4.   5.

BUBBLE TROUBLE

Billy loves a big bubble bath! He's taken lots of fun things into the tub — and one thing that has pretty sharp teeth!

Scan the scene and search for:

- a bar of soap
- a boat with a flag
- 7 crabs
- 7 ducks
- an octopus
- 10 popping bubbles
- a shark
- a spider
- 8 starfish
- 7 toothbrushes

KEEPING COOL!

```
t  h  w  d  w  q  f  q  k  a  m  d  m  t  t
k  d  j  j  b  a  z  g  c  s  u  n  d  a  e
j  d  f  s  x  a  f  b  s  u  o  m  m  u  b
h  d  s  l  l  p  u  n  e  o  y  k  o  i  v
k  v  i  c  n  w  s  a  r  w  r  k  q  s  o
o  a  x  l  o  x  z  r  n  y  l  u  o  g  g
a  n  d  y  w  o  e  k  b  a  j  y  p  h  c
v  i  i  x  c  b  p  q  e  c  h  e  r  r  y
v  l  f  n  w  f  l  w  s  p  l  i  t  y  j
e  l  v  a  q  z  k  f  u  d  g  e  f  s  j
n  a  r  j  o  m  r  i  j  m  a  m  i  n  t
h  t  h  s  p  r  i  n  k  l  e  s  m  c  j
s  s  u  w  l  o  l  l  i  p  o  p  b  o  g
c  h  o  c  o  l  a  t  e  g  e  w  a  n  a
b  l  t  z  z  h  k  d  l  n  s  y  h  e  y
```

SEARCH the grid to **FIND** all the **ICE CREAM** words below.

banana
bowl
cherry
chocolate

cone
fudge
lollipop
mint

scoop
split
sprinkles
strawberry

sundae
syrup
vanilla
wafer

BEWARE OF BEARS!

Find **FIVE** animals that are disguised as **BEARS**.

FOUND IT! The 5 animals are:

1. ⎯⎯⎯⎯⎯
2. ⎯⎯⎯⎯⎯
3. ⎯⎯⎯⎯⎯
4. ⎯⎯⎯⎯⎯
5. ⎯⎯⎯⎯⎯

WHO BLEW OUT THE CAMPFIRE?

Let's FIND who did it! LOOK at the list below and CROSS OUT the people who DON'T have each feature. Keep going until you have ONE person left – that's the CULPRIT!

The culprit has all of these features:

1. belt
2. spear
3. beard
4. brown jacket
5. headband

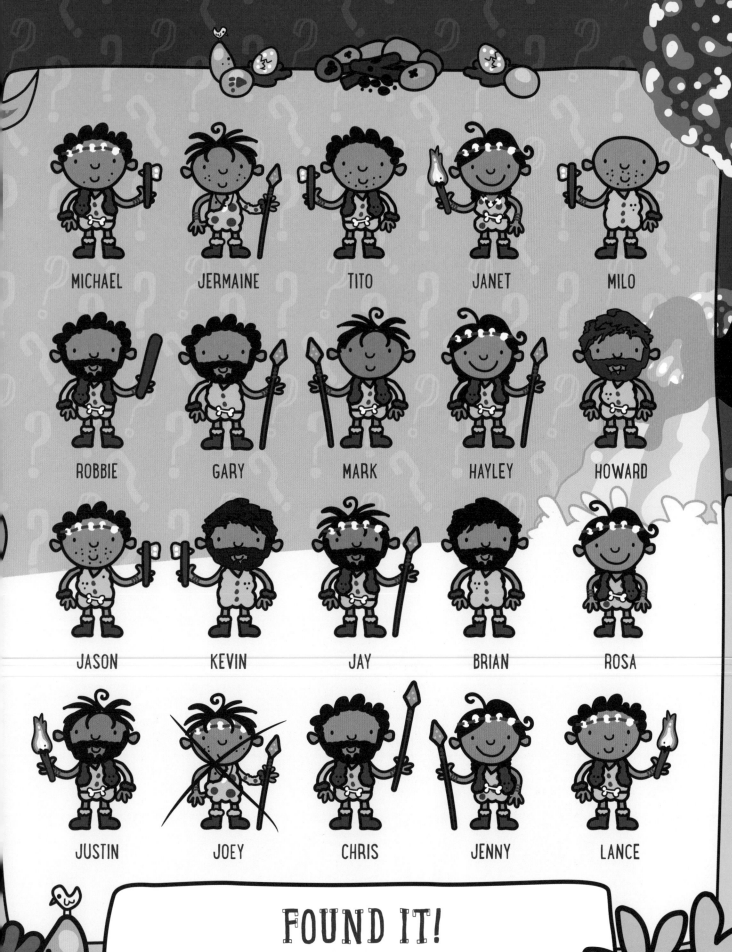

FOUND IT!

The culprit is ....

FIND THE DIFFERENCES!

Can you **FIND ALL FIVE DIFFERENCES** between the two pictures? Circle the differences on the right-hand page.

PET SHOP IN A PANIC!

The animals have escaped from their cages and now they're running wild! I wonder how they got out . . .

Scan the scene and search for:

- 4 bones
- 3 bows
- 8 cats
- 8 dogs
- 4 guinea pigs
- a heart
- a hole in the wall
- 4 mice
- a paw print
- 7 rabbits

FOLLOW THE TRAILS!

HELP the ALIEN choose the right trail to get to his FRIENDS.

FIND the picture that answers the **SUM.**

PIECE OF CAKE!

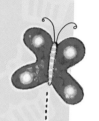

```
r g o y q n t c r t j o v e n
t e p m o e c o z l b d l f v
v d f r s l a c j h l u f r s
g q p a d j r o b h u p l o p
x a i k r t a n b p e y o s o
s k c a s l m u u l b i u t n
s i i j c v e t t v e q r i g
g u n y f a l a t e r c b n e
v e g g s n e h e l r v s g z
v e s a e i m w r w y s s e d
l e p a r l o y p v g u d x k
b a g m m l n u l c r e a m s
i d z f e a s p a r k l e s l
o c s u c u p c a k e x j w q
o t c s u z b m w o p s v d r
```

SEARCH the grid to FIND all the BAKING words below.

apron	coconut	flour	sparkles
blueberry	cream	frosting	sponge
butter	cupcake	lemon	sugar
caramel	eggs	oven	vanilla

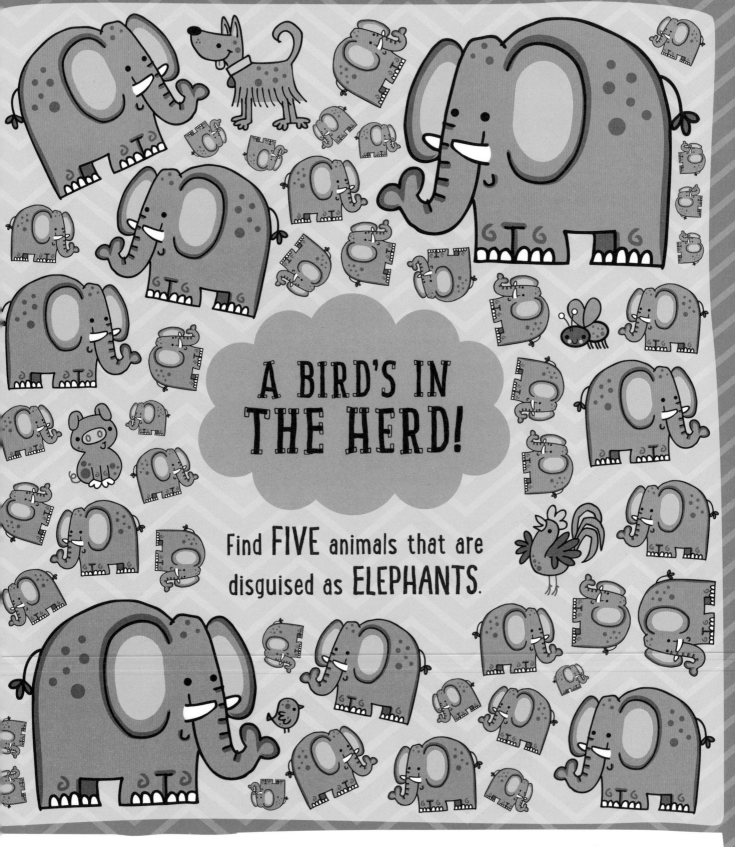

A BIRD'S IN THE HERD!

Find **FIVE** animals that are disguised as **ELEPHANTS**.

FOUND IT! The 5 animals are:

1. _____ 2. _____ 3. _____ 4. _____ 5. _____

RIDDLE ME THIS!

THE PIRATES WANT TREASURE!

The treasure is HIDDEN under one of the things on the ISLAND MAP. Solve the RIDDLE, then circle where you THINK you will find the treasure.

N

RIDDLE

You won't find me out in space —
I live in a much wetter place.

| A = ♥ |
| B = ♫ |
| C = ★ |
| D = ✔ |
| E = ✉ |
| F = ⚙ |
| G = ⌂ |
| H = 🔒 |
| I = ⚑ |
| J = 📕 |
| K = 🎁 |
| L = 💼 |
| M = 📌 |
| N = ✅ |
| O = 🔨 |
| P = 🚚 |
| Q = 🌐 |
| R = ✂ |
| S = 🍴 |
| T = 🚀 |
| U = ⚓ |
| V = 🔧 |
| W = 🔔 |
| X = 🗑 |
| Y = 🚀 |
| Z = ↺ |

CODE BREAKER

Now use the symbol chart to break
the code and find the answer:

🍴 🚀 ♥ ✂ ⚙ ⚑ 🍴 🔒

_____

ROADBLOCK AHEAD!

The busy workmen have caused a big traffic jam, but the kids on the bus don't mind because they might miss P.E.!

Scan the scene and search for:

- a ball
- a banana
- a bumblebee
- 3 daffodils
- a dinosaur
- 2 ducks
- an elephant
- a helmet
- a hole
- a letter

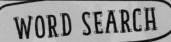

MERMAID MAYHEM!

```
n r m l t k y y v f i s h u b
s o r d d b k z r n m t m t l
e c h o n d y q r i l d e a j
a k y l e y g d y j x c r x b
w s s p m v e v f q a o h q b
e j e h e i t w l l c w x p p
e z p i r h l k a j n c a h e
d s q n m i d p n a l f k o a
y a g a a b c a e z k i c r i
e n t t i p m c y w x k n k x
e d c v d r o l m s h h a h w
b u t b e p l g l n k a o t a
p f a m k e p e a r l s l p v
q r h h h i v s e h l a z e e
c g r s l z n d g j v p f r p
```

SEARCH the grid to FIND all the MERMAID'S words below.

coral

crab

dolphin

fish

mermaid

merman

ocean

palace

pearl

rocks

sand

seaweed

shell

tail

whale

wave

MATCH THE PAIRS!

Draw lines to **JOIN** the matching **PAIRS OF SEA CREATURES**. Can you find all **FIVE** matching pairs?

UP, UP, AND AWAY!

Find **FIVE THINGS** that **DON'T BELONG.**

FOUND IT! The five things that don't belong are:

① ② ③ ④ ⑤

Circling in space is where I'll be.
You use me to get great TV!

A = ♥
B = ♪
C = ★
D = ✔
E = ✉
F = ⚙
G = 🏠
H = 🔒
I = 🚩
J = 📕
K = 🎁
L = 💼
M = 📌
N = ✅
O = 🔨
P = 🚚
Q = 🌎
R = ✂
S = 🍴
T = 🚀
U = ⚓
V = 🔧
W = 🔔
X = 🗑
Y = 🚀
Z = ↺

CODE BREAKER

Now use the symbol chart to break
the code and find the answer:

🍴 ♥ 🚀 ✉ 💼 💼 🚩 🚀 ✉

_____ _____ _____ _____ _____ _____ _____ _____ _____

THE FAST TRACK

Everyone is going for gold on the athletic track, but there are lots of strange things going on that make winning pretty tricky . . .

Scan the scene and search for:

- an apple
- an astronaut
- a crocodile
- an elephant
- an ice-cream cone
- an igloo
- a prize goat
- a sand castle
- a strong mouse
- a tired person

KITTY-CAT CONFUSION!

Find **FIVE** animals that are disguised as **CATS**.

FOUND IT! The 5 animals are:

1. ____ 2. ____ 3. ____ 4. ____ 5. ____

FIND a way through the MAZE to help the
EMERGENCY workers find their VEHICLES.
Try to HELP at each emergency on the way!

TO THE
RESCUE!

START 2

START 1

FINISH 2

FINISH 1

FOREST FIASCO

The busy campers left their campsite alone for too long and now it is overrun with animals! Are you brave enough to get the tea kettle back?

Scan the scene and search for:

- 6 acorns
- 2 badgers
- 2 campers
- 2 deer
- 4 ducks
- 4 mice
- a sleeping owl
- 4 snails
- a spider
- 6 toadstools

FOLLOW THE TRAILS!

HELP the RABBIT choose the right trail to get to the CARROTS.

PICK A PRINCESS!

FIND the picture that answers the SUM.

PUMPKIN PARTY!

```
l  n  b  s  g  c  f  t  r  i  c  k  a  l  u
c  c  r  p  t  o  p  y  p  a  r  t  y  a  c
a  h  n  i  x  s  i  v  z  u  b  n  u  q  r
n  x  j  d  a  t  l  z  o  f  s  a  g  s  e
d  a  j  e  y  u  d  f  c  a  k  f  t  r  e
y  l  w  r  h  m  j  o  z  l  e  k  x  a  p
n  i  f  i  q  e  b  u  c  n  l  c  m  r  y
g  g  h  m  n  f  t  m  f  c  e  l  x  s  b
e  q  g  f  j  d  u  c  i  s  t  a  n  b  v
m  d  n  z  u  j  h  n  k  d  o  z  p  a  t
p  u  m  p  k  i  n  d  c  a  n  d  l  e  s
r  x  e  v  g  r  d  u  x  y  f  i  h  a  i
t  r  e  a  t  b  l  i  n  p  w  r  g  w  e
i  q  t  z  s  u  r  p  r  i  s  e  y  h  b
c  t  o  e  c  y  h  w  u  l  g  h  c  a  t
```

SEARCH the grid to FIND all the FAIRY'S words below.

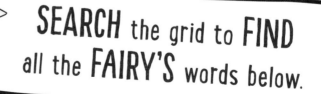

bat
candles
candy
cat

costume
creepy
fun
midnight

party
pumpkin
skeleton
spider

surprise
treat
trick
wind

BUSY BAKERS!

FIND the picture that answers the **SUM**.

KATE WILLIAM GEORGE HARRY ANDREW

ELIZABETH ANN PHILLIP LARRY MONICA

BARRY PIP OSCAR BERT ERNIE

ROSS CHANDLER RACHEL PHOEBE JOEY

FOUND IT!

The culprit is ....

FOLLOW THE TRAILS!

HELP the FAIRY choose the right trail to get to the ICE-CREAM CONES.

SNOW-WHERE TO HIDE!

Find **FIVE** animals that are disguised as **POLAR BEARS**.

FOUND IT! The 5 animals are:

1. _____

2. _____

3. _____

4. _____

5. _____

FARMER FRANK HAS LOST HIS KEYS!

Frank's keys are **HIDDEN** under one of the animal pens on the **FARM MAP.** Solve the **RIDDLE**, then circle where you **THINK** you will find the keys.

RIDDLE

I don't have feet; I have no toes, yet I wear shoes wherever I go.

Symbol chart:

A = ♥
B = ♪
C = ★
D = ✔
E = ✉
F = ⚙
G = 🏠
H = 🔒
I = 🚩
J = 📕
K = 🎁
L = 💼
M = 📌
N = ✔
O = 🔨
P = 🚚
Q = 🌐
R = ✂
S = 🍴
T = ✈
U = ⚓
V = 🔧
W = 🔔
X = 🗑
Y = 🚀
Z = ↺

CODE BREAKER

Now use the symbol chart to break the code and find the answer:

🔒 🔨 ✂ 🍴 ✉

_____ _____ _____ _____ _____

CIRCUS SHOW!

```
o  l  a  u  g  h  d  t  p  c  s  k  z  d  h
u  c  l  o  w  n  w  e  l  e  p  h  a  n  t
r  f  d  o  l  e  l  i  o  n  n  c  r  b  e
i  v  d  p  s  k  i  r  q  o  b  c  o  n  n
n  c  i  a  f  h  m  g  n  v  e  a  l  u  t
g  h  r  u  u  e  i  n  h  x  y  c  l  e  l
c  w  s  d  i  l  a  l  e  t  h  r  e  k  a
c  c  e  i  i  c  n  d  h  t  s  o  r  b  z
t  i  r  e  n  g  x  a  p  t  n  b  c  j  i
f  o  r  n  x  g  e  n  l  n  x  a  o  h  c
o  p  l  c  f  j  l  c  a  d  w  t  a  j  h
o  e  p  e  u  e  b  e  t  b  y  u  s  l  f
f  n  u  f  y  s  u  g  e  z  j  k  t  j  p
n  c  h  e  e  r  l  v  s  k  d  u  e  b  s
o  k  n  c  m  b  e  i  e  e  g  t  r  b  i
```

SEARCH the grid to FIND all the CIRCUS FAIRIES' words below.

acrobat	circus	laugh	roller coaster
audience	clown	lion	sing
cannon	dance	plates	tent
cheer	elephant	ring	weights

FIND THE DIFFERENCES!

THINGS THAT DON'T BELONG!

MISSION ON THE MOON!
The five things that don't belong are:
- builder
- cow
- crab
- dinosaur
- rooster

UP, UP, AND AWAY
The five things that don't belong are:
- alien
- dinosaur
- rooster
- sheep
- zebra

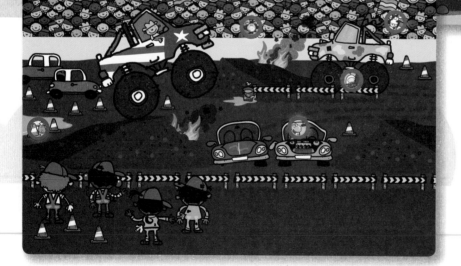

ROUND THE BEND
The five things that don't belong are:
- alien
- cow
- dinosaur
- pig
- sheep

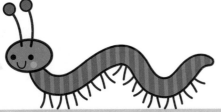

UNDERWATER UNDERCOVER!

The five things that don't belong are:

- bee
- Dalmatian
- mouse
- peacock
- sheep

HIDING ON-SITE!

The five things that don't belong are:

- alien
- caveman
- dinosaur
- sheep
- astronaut

STRANGE SAFARI

The five things that don't belong are:

- dinosaur
- igloo
- pig
- polar bear
- sheep

PATTERN DISGUISES!

EARN YOUR STRIPES!
dog, mouse, pig, poodle, rabbit

EARN YOUR STRIPES!

Find **FIVE** animals that are disguised as TIGERS.

SOMETHING'S FISHY!
crab, jellyfish, sea horse, starfish, turtle

SOMETHING'S FISHY!

Find **FIVE** animals that are disguised as spotted FISH.

A BIRD'S IN THE HERD!
bee, bird, rooster, dog, pig

A BIRD'S IN THE HERD!

Find **FIVE** animals that are disguised as ELEPHANTS.

SEEING STRIPES!
bug, dog, goat, polar bear, toucan

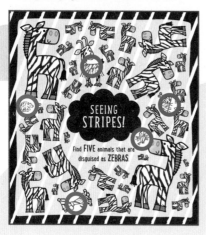

SEEING STRIPES!

Find **FIVE** animals that are disguised as ZEBRAS.

KITTY-CAT CONFUSION!
caterpillar, cow, dog, rabbit, shark

KITTY-CAT CONFUSION!

Find **FIVE** animals that are disguised as CATS.

IT'S A DOG'S LIFE!
chick, hamster, rabbit, rhino, snail

WHO IS MOO?
duck, frog, goose, mouse, sheep

SNOW-WHERE TO HIDE!
elephant, hippo, lion, rhino, sheep

WONDERFUL WINGS
ant, bee, parrot, puffer fish, spider

BEWARE OF BEARS!
cat, caterpillar, crab, crocodile, sea lion

MATCH THE PAIRS!

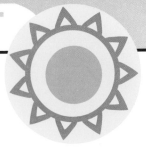

MATCH THE PAIRS!

Draw lines to JOIN the matching PAIRS OF ANIMALS. Can you find all FIVE matching pairs?

MATCH THE PAIRS!

Draw lines to JOIN the matching PAIRS OF SEA CREATURES. Can you find all FIVE matching pairs?

MATCH THE PAIRS!

Draw lines to JOIN the matching PAIRS AT THE BEACH. Can you find the FIVE matching pairs?

MATCH THE PAIRS!

Draw lines to JOIN the matching PAIRS AT THE PARTY. Can you find all FIVE matching pairs?

VISUAL SUMS

I SCREAM FOR ICE CREAM!

FIND the picture that answers the SUM.

CUPCAKE CONFUSION!

FIND the picture that answers the SUM.

ROCKING RABBITS!

FIND the picture that answers the SUM.

CLOTHING CALCULATION!

FIND the picture that answers the SUM.

MIXED-UP MATEYS!

FIND the picture that answers the SUM.

PICK A PRINCESS!

FIND the picture that answers the SUM.

BUSY BAKERS!

FIND the picture that answers the SUM.

MAZES!

BUG BUDDIES

FIND a way through the MAZE to help the BUTTERFLY get to its CATERPILLAR friend. Try not to bump into the other BUGS on the way!

START

FINISH

MAJESTIC MAZE

FIND a way through the MAZE to help the PRINCE get to the PRINCESS. Try to pick up the JEWELS on the way!

START

FINISH

ROCKET RACE

FIND a way through the MAZE to help the ROCKET get to EARTH. Try not to bump into the COMETS on the way!

START

FINISH

FIND a way through the MAZE to help the
EMERGENCY workers find their VEHICLES.
Try to HELP at each emergency on the way!

TO THE RESCUE!

START 1

START 2

FINISH 2

FINISH 1

FIND a way through the MAZE to help
the FARMER find her LOST SHEEP.
Try to pick up all the SHEEP on the way!

COUNTING SHEEP!

START

FINISH

WORD SEARCHES

PERFECT PALACE
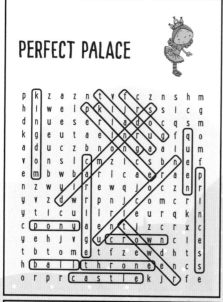

```
p k z a z n t y f c z n s h m
h d l w e l p k j r s l c g
d k n g u e s e r l a d o c q
k a g e u t a e l n r u g f
a v o u c z b n o n g a i a
e n n s l c m z i c s b n
n z w u l r e w q j o c z
y t l c u a e n t j z c r
c p o n y a e n t j z c r
y e h z t o m e t f z e w
h b t o m e t f z e w n
h b a l l t h r o n e
o r p r c a s t l e
```

PIECE OF CAKE!
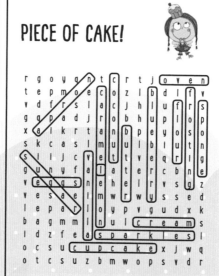

```
r g o y g n t c r t o v e n
t e p m o o e a c a i u d
v d f r s l a c h l f r
g q p a d j m o u e l o
x a i k r t a h h b y s
s k c a s t b u l e r p
s l l j c v m t e b r o
g u n y f a n e m e r n
v e s a e o m o r r y
l e p a r t l o y p v
b d z f e a s i n u l c r e a m
l d z f e a s p a r k l e s
o c s a z m w o p s v d
o t c s u z b m w o p s v d
```

MERMAID MAYHEM!

```
n r m l t k y y f i s h u b
s e a r h y s e d o l e d
w r o c k s j z p h i m e d e a
a w e e j z s a p i m r e w o x t
e d z c v a i t o r o l m s h h a h
b u t f a m k e p e a r l s l p
p r h h v s z l i n d g j v p f r p
c g r s l z n d g j v p f r p
```

KEEPING COOL

```
t h w d w g f q k a m d m t t
k d j j a z g c s u n d a e
j d f s x a f s u o m m u b
h d c s l p u n e o v k o h
k o l l c n w s a r w r k q s o
a l n d y w o e k a j y o g
v v l f n w f l w s p l i t y
e l a r j o m r l j m a m i n t
n a r j o m r l j m a m i n t
h t h s p r i n k l e s m o
s u w l o l l i p o p b o
c h o c o l a t e g e w a
h l t z z h k d l n s y h e y
```

SEARCHING SPACE!
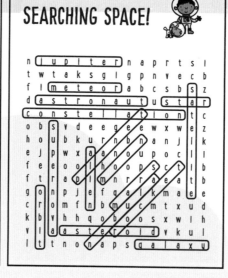

```
n j u p i t e r n a p r t s l
t w t a k s g l g p n v e c b
f l m e t e o r a b c s b s
d a s t r o n a u t u s t a r
c o n s t e l l a t i o n t
o b s v d e e g e w x w t e l
h o j u b k u r n h a n o u p o c l t
f e r e o l h o o p s j t l
f t m n r r a e l x m
g o p j e f g a l k m a
c r o m f n b m u c m x t u d
k u t h q o b o o s x w l h
l l a s t e r o i d v k u l
l t n o n a p s g a l a x y
```

SEE THE SITES!
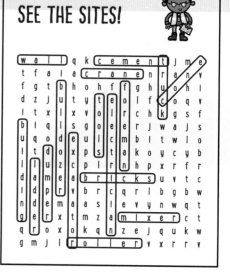

```
w a l q k c e m e n t j m e
t f a i a c r a n e r a n y
f g t b h o h f f g t u o h
z j u l t x g u l e r c h q
b u u o t e o r e m h o k
l o x d z e x c a t e o
l d z e x c a t e o
d u m b r i c k s u v e
i u t o l d z e q n d
n m z a m i x e r c t
g m j r o l l e r v x r r v
```

FARMYARD FUN!

```
d b t g r k m b a r n f n r
y k t t v v m c t e w f t w
f l s t a b l e s k c a q o
g l c t q c a e g s u y r a
a t a j h o v l l e a c v e
r c l p x r h j l e a i y c
m e o t o n r d t r c s o t
e f n u e z s k w l s d u d
r g d e g g m e a d o w p a
s h e p h e r d a p k d c n q
u v i k c a e u l a m d t m h
d u x g e e v r x o q c o r n
c g o o s e t l o v x n r a s
```

FINDING FOSSILS!

```
n y u m w r g c j z g q e r w
o f m b d o b l l w d y i d f
u q a v z s k b e i w o f y f
u a g e n a r c l a f r o m t
m e e n a j t e r o d a e r i
e t i f f w a t o n t o s u r
t p f a b e h l t e d c c n i
v o t o g i m e o o s e o r c
o l r u u l u t t l a g h q e
l c y u l y l u z y a k n u r
u m w b b m u r g o s m f t o
n o k b h h h s d h c t k s p
```

CIRCUS SHOW!

```
o l a u g h d t p c s k z d h
r l f d o l e l l o n n c r e
i l v d p s k l c l a f m o l
n h r u e l h m n s v l l e e
g r e d l l a t o u l e r b p
t l r e n g x a n b a r o h
o e p e u e b e t s u e t z f
f n u f y s u g e l x d u e b
o k n c m b e l e e e e g t l
c h e e r l v e l d u e r l
```

MIGHTY MACHINES!

```
m x s m i r r o r t y v s d l
m e c h a n i c o r g u j r l
w t x v l j l v u y f c a v t s
h o p e q c a r k b u n w v e
w a r z j t q z d n e u k e a
g g m k u l n p w p l h k t
z y j m s t o o l b o x h p n
b t c a u e h o f k l l s x m e
v l a r u s r o u e m u s u l r
b g r v t e m p r t u x x f o
w h e e l n w w t r u c k a s f l
h w r o a d y w o m n d p x d v j x
e y b h r u l s c o n e o
l y b v e h i c l e g c y c
d o v o v e o i l s g v
```

HIDDEN TREASURE!

```
g h l g g r o g t o s w o r d
d x a p t q c o i n s q a z g
a l h a g o i l u p p b l b t
f w o r l x n d a z r o q z
m b w r g l e l v n l a a d
p j b a u q u e n d a s k
o a b t d l q u a t o l u l
f t p g r b o n e s v l h
a a c a n n o n t y s z u l
m o s d v w l l s v j c
b t p e l s o l v h q v n s j
b f k t g p z t r e a s u r e
t e e q x o u y h d q l c v j
o q t x a c b u r i e d p x y
```

PUMPKIN PARTY!

```
l n b s g c f t r i c k a l u
c c r p t o p y p a r t u a c
a n x j d a s t l z o f s a g s
a j e y u d c a n k f t r e
l w r h m j o z l e k x a p
g g h m n f m f c l x s b v
m d n z u j m u c i n m a t y
p u m p k i n d c a n d l e s
r x e v g r d u x y f h a l
t r e a t b l n p w r g w e
l q t z s u r p r i s e y h b
c t o e c y h w u l g h c a t
```

RIDDLE ME THIS!

DINO DAVE IS LOOKING FOR FOOD!

Dave's food is hidden under the:
- volcano

_____

MECHANIC MIKE HAS LOST HIS HAMMER!

Mike's hammer is hidden under the:
- police car

_____

THE PIRATES WANT TREASURE!

The treasure is hidden under the:
- starfish

_____

THE ASTRONAUT HAS LOST HIS DOG!

The dog is hidden under the:
- satellite

_____

THE POLAR BEAR HAS LOST HER CUB!

The cub is hidden under the:
- igloo

_____

FARMER FRANK HAS LOST HIS KEYS!

Frank's keys are hidden under the:
- horse

_____

THE GOLD MEDALS ARE MISSING!

The medals are hidden under the:

· sports bag

_____

PRINCESS PIPPA HAS LOST HER TIARA!

The tiara is hidden under the:

· knight

_____

A THIEF HAS ESCAPED!

The thief is hiding in the:

· hospital

_____

LARRY THE LION HAS LOST HIS PRIDE!

Larry's pride is hidden under the:

· elephant

_____

FIND THE CULPRIT!

WHO BLEW OUT THE CAMPFIRE?

The culprit is:
- Jay

WHO ATE BUILDER BILL'S LUNCH?

The culprit is:
- Ryan

WHO ATE ALL OF THE PET FOOD?

The culprit is:
- Rosie

WHO LEFT THE GARAGE IN SUCH A MESS?

The culprit is:
- Doug

WHO LET THE ANIMALS ESCAPE?

The culprit is:
- Ricky

WHO STOLE THE GOLD MEDAL?

The culprit is:
- Elizabeth